This book belongs to

_____

To sweet, little Muslims everywhere.

LITTLE MUSLIMS
BIG QUESTIONS

Who is Allah?

"Who is Allah?" The Little Muslim asked the ants marching by.

"Who is Allah?"
He asked the birds flying by.

But no one answered ...

Until the rain clouds settled in,
and all the animals gathered under
the old willow tree,
that's when they all sang gleefully:

"Allah is our Creator, He made you and me.
He made everything as far as our eyes can see."

"Allah hears, sees, and knows all,
He is always near whenever we call."

"Allah does not eat, nor does He sleep. He is our one true friend, who we must always keep."

"Allah loves and cares for each one of us."

"His promise is of Jannah, and He will never abandon us!"

...So where is Allah?
Read the next, 'Little Muslims, Big Questions'
book to find out!

Published in the local newspaper for winning a regional writing competition at 16, Sana knew exactly what she wanted to do when she grew up – become an author. When Sana realized the need for Muslim literature and representation in mainstream children's books, she set out to fulfill her childhood dream by penning the 'Little Muslims, Big Questions,' series inspired by her beautiful daughters and their wonder for Islam.

Sana currently resides in Toronto, Canada with her family.

www.ingramcontent.com/pod-product-compliance
Lightning Source LLC
Chambersburg PA
CBHW040210100526
44585CB00002BA/100